Beir Bua Press - Kids

www.BeirBuaPress.com

Elephants Sleep in Bunk Beds

by

Carl Burkitt

Published by Beir Bua Press

For Frank and Caroline

ISBN: 978-1-914972-31-7

Beir Bua Press, Co. Tipperary, Ireland.

Typesetting / Layout, Cover Design and background image: Michelle Moloney King.

Ordering Information: For details, see www.BeirBuaPress.com

Published by Beir Bua Press. Printed in the UK - Our printer is certified as a B Corporation to measure our impact on the environment and help drive us to be even more conscious of our footprint.

9 781914 972317

Elephants Sleep in Bunk Beds

Carl Burkitt

THE START

A book will stay a mystery
until you look inside.
By staring at the cover
you don't know what you'll find.

There could be seven tigers
with red and purple stripes.
There could be thirteen donkeys
riding chocolate bikes.

There could be distant planets
where polar bears can talk
and all the fruits and vegetables
grow legs so they can walk.

There could be fish with glasses
and sharks in woolly hats.
There could be singing dinosaurs
and football playing bats.

There could be things unheard of
to shock and thrill your heart.
So come on in, turn the page
and let the tales start.

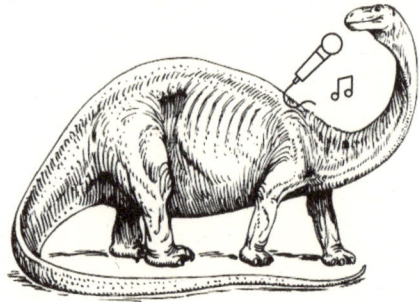

FAMOUSLY

The fox and the baboon
the ox and the racoon

the beaver and the pug
the retriever and the slug

the lamb and the chinchilla
the ram and the gorilla

the hen and the Alsatian
the wren and the crustacean

the bear and the eagle
the hare and the beagle

the eel and the snail
the seal and the whale

the goose and the louse
the moose and the mouse

the moth and the vole
the sloth and the mole

the frog and the bee
the hog and the flea

all went out for tea
and got on famously.

I KNOW! I KNOW!

Hands up, said the teacher.
Which creature has a long pink neck and wings?
I know! I know! said Antonio. **A rhino!**
Um… no, said the teacher. *A flamingo.*

Hands up, said the teacher.
Which creature has tiny scales but bulging eyes?
I know! I know! said Antonio. **A rhino!**
Um… no, said the teacher. *A gecko!*

Hands up, said the teacher.
Which creature has small ears, large teeth and swims?
I know! I know! said Antonio. **A rhino!**
Um… no, said the teacher. *A hippo!*

Hands up, said the teacher.
Which creature has a miniature body and sucks human blood?
I know! I know! said Antonio. **A rhino!**
Um… no, said the teacher. *A mosquito!*

Hands up, said the teacher.
Which creature has one sharp pointy horn on its head?
I know! I know! said Antonio. **A bunny!**
Wait, what? No, said the teacher. *A rhino!*

FISH FINGERS

Phillip had fish fingers.
Not the breaded kind
you have with chips and peas
and sometimes beans.

Oh no no no.

Phillip's fish fingers were the alive kind.
The ones with tails and gills
and flapped through oceans and tides.

Make no mistake,
Phillip's fish fingers were not on his plate,
Phillip's fish fingers were on his hands.

I really, really need you to understand.
Phillip had fingers…that were actual fish.

One wave from him was hard to miss.

RARE OCTOPUS

Graeme woke this morning
with eight tentacles for arms.
He used one to rub his tired eyes,
one to switch off his alarm.

He used two for wrapping presents,
two to bake a chocolate cake,
then he went to his friend's birthday
and used the last to hug his mate.

BUMBLE

There's a scary looking bee
sitting on my toilet roll.

Perhaps it's pooped some honey
and needs to wipe its bumble.

PICNIC DISASTER

The sausage rolled down the hill.
The butternut squashed the
sandwiches.
The apple turned over the table.

The potato mashed up the crisps.
The chocolate caked the blanket in mud.
The banana split the carton of juice.

The raspberry jammed the basket shut.
The caramel waffled on for ever and ever.
All in all, it was an utter picnic disaster.

FACTS

Pigs like rubbing honey on their tummy skin.
Monkeys like cheese cut incredibly thin.

A leopard won't eat breakfast unless there's scrambled eggs.
Pandas enjoy sleeping standing upright on three legs.

Elephants and humans are the only creatures with a chin.
A penguin trained for the Olympics but didn't make it in.

Bears use bats for hanging washing instead of little pegs.
Pigeons like swimming in half full beer kegs.

Rhinos can't stop sneezing from one speck of dust.
If a cow gets too wet they have been known to rust.

A butterfly is made of over 50,000 ribs.
Nothing scares a lion more than babies in their cribs.

A giraffe can juggle chainsaws if it really must.
Zebras can't keep secrets, they're unreliable to trust.

When tigers eat their dinner they all wear tiny bibs.
Only one of these facts is true, the rest are total fibs.

HAIR

Daniel let his hair grow.
It covered both his eyes.
He couldn't see in front of him,
he couldn't see the skies.

It tickled both his ear holes,
his cheeks and mouth and nose,
it tickled both his nipples
as it grew down to his toes.

A DOLPHIN IN THE SHOPS

I saw a dolphin in the shops today.
I promise, I'm telling the truth.
There were lobsters working on the tills
and a shark cleaning the roof.

I saw a dolphin in the shops today.
It sounds unreal but it's true.
There were starfish pushing trolleys
and an octopus buying fruit.

I saw a dolphin in the shops today,
it felt like something from a dream.
There were squids down the biscuit aisle
and whales in the ice cream.

ELEPHANTS SLEEP IN BUNK BEDS

Elephants dislike lowdown beds,
elephants prefer a bunk.

The top is used for their bottom,
the bottom is used for their trunk.

AS STRONG AS AN ANT

Ants can carry twenty times their body weight.
If humans could do that, wouldn't it be great?!

I'd give my closest friends the world's biggest piggyback,
I'd drag cars and trucks around like Father Christmas in a sack.

I'd juggle 50 bowling balls, pick up mountains when I saw them.
I'd play basketball with elephants, lift up planets to fight boredom.

Do you know what you would do with ant-like strength?
I would carry all my family everywhere I went.

PUDDLE MUDDLE

The puppy saw a puppy in a puddle
It sent her mind into a muddle
She got soaking wet
When their noses met
Going in for a big, sloppy cuddle

A MOMENT OF MAGIC

The little egg cracked in the middle of spring
and out popped a chick with a beak and two wings.

Its eyes were wide and its feet had claws
and it looked around at things on the floor.

It looked at the squirrels, it looked at the trees,
it looked at the bunnies and the flowers with bees.

It looked at the cats, it looked at the dogs,
it looked at the pond with the toads and the frogs.

It looked at the badgers, it looked at the moles,
it looked at the mud and the worms making holes.

It looked at the grass, it looked at the river,
then it looked at the sky and began to shiver.

The big stretch of blue put a buzz in its tummy,
its body felt warm and its feathers felt fuzzy.

The ground was pretty and as fun as could be
but the chick could feel it had somewhere else to be.

It stretched its legs and unfurled its wings
as a moment of magic was about to begin:

a moment of beauty, a moment up high,
a moment of joy as the chick learned to fly.

HONEY PARSNIP

Honey Parsnip was a very sweet girl,
the sweetest girl in the whole wide world.

She loved giving hugs but they were a little bit icky
because her skin and her limbs were so awfully sticky.

TRAFFIC JAM ON THE FARM

The cow said *Moooooove!*
The horse said *Neeeeeeigh-body can move!*

The sheep said *This is baaaaaad!*
The sheepdog said *Woof's going on?!*

The pig said *Oink have no idea what's going on!*
The chicken said *We're cluck in a standstill!*

The duck said *Quack quack quack quack!*
which didn't really make any sense.

HARRY'S SKIPPING ROPE

Harry had his skipping rope one afternoon
He jumped and jumped whistling a tune
He jumped so high
Right into the sky
And landed on the far away moon

CAN YOU IMAGINE?

You've seen an ant before, yeah?
And you've seen a picture of an anteater before, yeah?

Well, have you ever seen an anteater-eater?
Or an anteater-eater-eater?

Or an anteater-eater-eater-eater?
Or an anteater-eater-eater-eater-eater?

Can you even begin to imagine what an anteater-
eater-eater-eater-eater-eater looks like?!

I can't either, but I bet it's pretty big,
much bigger than an ant.

COUNTING SHEEP

If you find it hard to get to sleep
people say *Try counting sheep.*

I don't do that, I count pigs.
The kind who wear bright purple wigs.

It doesn't help me start to snore,
I just find counting sheep a bore.

A MILLION BAGS

Lexie popped her shoes on
and went shopping in the town.
There was nothing that she needed,
she just went for a browse.

Fast forward 20 minutes
and she had a *million* bags,
each one stuffed with goodies
from diamond rings to garlic crabs.

FOLLOW THESE INSTRUCTIONS
WHEN YOU READ THIS POEM

Pat your head when you read this line
Rub your tummy when you read this line
Pretend you're an egg when you read this line
Yell the word *YUMMY* when you read this line

Clap your hands when you read this line
Stick out your tongue when you read this line
Sit don't stand when you read this line
Stick up your thumb when you read this line

Tap your thighs when you read this line
Buzz like a bee when you read this line
Close your eyes when you read the *next* line
Don't read this, I said close your eyes!

YOU KNOW!

The other day I was chatting to that pig.
    You know, the one with the wig.
    The wig that's too big
    and made of figs and bits of twigs.

You know, the pig,
he's friends with that goat.
The goat with the tiny boat
made of dusty coats and TV remotes.

You know, the goat and the pig,
they hang out with that cow.
The cow with the eyebrows
made of snow ploughs and know how.

You know, the cow and the goat and the pig,
they're always chatting to that duck.
The duck with the monster truck
made of hockey pucks and dog muck.

You know, the duck and the cow and the goat and the
pig,
they're buddies with that horse.
The horse with the racecourse
made of brute force and tomato sauce.

You know, the horse and the duck
and the cow and the goat and the pig!!!
You know, maybe you haven't met.
I mean, they're pretty hard to forget.

ARTY CHOKE

Arty Choke was an interesting bloke
made of a thousand different layers.

He wrote romance novels and told silly jokes,
he was a nurse, a DJ and champion chess player.

He wore cargo shorts and a bright yellow cloak,
his eyebrows were black, his beard was greyer.

He was charming and shy, people loved when he spoke,
so the town cast a vote: *Arty Choke to be Mayor.*

CLIP CLOP

Chloe's
    caterpillar
        clapped its
            countless
                clogs
                    clip clop
                        across the
                            kitchen floor
                        clip clop
                    before
                  backtracking
                back to the
              back garden
            brandishing a
          bucket load of
    bourbon
biscuits.

UNIQUE CREATURE FEATURES

DORMOUSE
This creature has legs
one, two, three, four,
but instead of a mouth
it has a food-munching door.

HORSE-FLY
This creature has wings
to fly through the room,
but instead of toes
it has miniature hooves.

HAMMERHEAD SHARK
This creature has fins
to help it swim,
but instead of teeth
it has nails knocked in.

EARWIG
This creature has claws
at the end of its legs,
but instead of hair
it has a toupee on its head.

BOTTLENOSE DOLPHIN
This creature has a blowhole
to breathe through its back,
but instead of nostrils
it has two bottle caps.

BULLDOG
This creature has cheeks
that fill up when it's fed,
but instead of curly ears
it has two horns on its head.

CATFISH
This creature has whiskers,
a hairy tail and wet nose,
but instead of fur
it has slippy skin on its bones.

HONEY BADGER
This creature has stripes
down its legs and arms,
but instead of its room
it has its bed in a jar.

BARN OWL
This creature has a beak
on its face like it should,
but instead of feathers
it has a body made of wood.

SPIDER MONKEY
This creature has a tail
to swing between trees,
but instead of two
it has eight separate knees.

ONE OF A KIND

Brodie was a special lad,
a true one of a kind.
He had a unique feature,
around the world you'd never find.

It wasn't his big smile
or his squishy, charming legs,
but the fact he was a human
with an onion for a head.

BAD WEATHER

It was a rainy day and the T-Rex was bored,
so it grabbed nail clippers to trim its claws.

Snip, snip, snip, it clipped two, three, four
and its ginormous nails rained down to the floor.

The nervous triceratops below eating veg
looked up when it felt something sharp on its head.

Don't be scared, old pal, the T-Rex said.
I'm just doing some grooming before going to bed.

Oh, right! the Triceratops said, a little alert.
The rain felt hard and I thought 'How absurd!'

Hard rain! Imagine that! the T-Rex laughed until it hurt
while the weather continued to get worse and worse.

Come here, the T-Rex said, holding its umbrella,
and the pair snuggled up to stay dry together.

PIRATE AT HOME

Captain Patricia was a ruthless pirate.
Other pirates would cower and cry if they saw her.

However no other pirate ever really did see her
because young Captain Patricia got sea sick out on the ocean.

So instead she spent her days commanding the land around her,
firing balled up paper from her arm-cannons across the lounge.

She pinched any penny she found down the sofa
and buried it in the back garden.

She secretly smuggled chocolates from the treat drawer
inside her homemade skull and bones paper hat.

Her parents wouldn't let her have pets
so she'd sit and smoulder with a carrot on her shoulder.

She threatened people on TV with her tin-foil hook
and made her teddy bears walk the plank into the bath.

Oh what a true brute Captain Patricia was to be known,
lucky for you and me she never left her home.

JACK FRUIT

Jack Fruit is such a hoot.
Feed him beans and watch him toot.
He loves to strum a lettuce lute
and only wears a carrot suit.

He lives inside an old tree root
with his pet, Clive the newt.
He drinks his tea from a recycled boot
and rather than wave, he gives a salute.

You'll never see the man in a car park dispute
because Jack doesn't drive things
that pollute.

ANIMAL SCHOOL

The cat learned to catch a frisbee
The shark learned to sharpen a
pencil
The bird learned to burp
The tiger learned to tie its shoelaces

The fox learned to foxtrot
The cow learned to count to 10
The goat learned to go to the toilet
The butterfly learned to butter its
bread

The spider learned to spy
The pig learned to pick its nose
The cuckoo learned to cook a meal
The rhino learned to ride a bike

ALARM CLOCK

I'm a snoozer, a snorer,
a morning yawner.
I'm a hibernating bear
without a care in the world.

I'm the best at lying down
with a soft pillow crown
for my big drowsy head
on my big cloudy bed.

I count sheep in my sleep
and I dream for weeks.
My duvet feels so heavy
if I wake before I'm ready.

So if you see the lights off
then you better not knock
and if you're an alarm clock
then you better switch off.

ANNE ONION

Anne Onion was a frightful lady
That really is no lie
She'd say mean things
And peel off her skin
To make other people cry

MR B. TROOT

Mr B. Troot was embarrassed
of his cheeks that glowed purple.

Every birthday he'd wish for a shell
to hide like a turtle.

But one day when he was older
and his reflection caught his eye,

he noticed purple was unique.
Wow, he thought. *How handsome am I?!*

WHAT IS A CARPET?

A carpet is hair for the ground.
It's a jumper for floorboards.
It's lava, so be careful.
It's a pitch for goals to be scored.

A carpet is a baseball glove for dog hair.
It's a million hugs for your toes.
It's soft tarmac for toy cars to drive on.
It's a tissue for the world's biggest nose.

A carpet is a furry ocean.
It's a forest of miniature trees.
It's the sky covered in crumbs.
It's anything you want it to be.

THE WARMEST CHILD

Seth never wore a jumper,
a scarf or hat or gloves.
His skin would never feel the chill
and cold he never was.

He wore his shorts in winter
with no shoes in the snow,
he was the warmest child
the world had ever known.

WHAT DID THEY HAVE FOR LUNCH?

Ed had bread.
Jean had beans.
Ash had mashed potatoes.

Pip had chips.
Kate had cake.
Lucy had juicy grapes.

Lee had peas.
Steve had cheese.
Tom had tomatoes.

Peter had fajitas.
Claire had eclairs.
Charlie had pastrami.

Clive had chives and pies and fries
and a helping of strudel with egg fried rice...
you know what Clive's like.

ETERNITY

I
wrote
a
poem
so
long
and
thin,
it
was
such
a
thrill,
exhilaratin'.
I
could
have
kept
on
writing
for
eternity,
an
age,
until
all
of
a
sudden
I
ran
out
of
page...

PEACH SLICE

Peach Slice was not very nice.

She'd lure people in
with her soft, sweet skin

then pinch their bike
and steal their phone

because smiling Peach Slice
had a heart of stone.

.

CHRISTMAS SECRET

Mistletoes grow
on mistlefeet trees.

QUIETLY IN THE EVENING

Have you ever heard
a bird sing at night?
It's usually in the morning
when they tweet their delight.

Except for the owls,
who like to twit-twoo
quietly in the evening
so they don't wake you.

A CHEF A-Z

Aaron's avocado was ace
Billy's beans were brilliant
Colin's coconuts were class

Donna's doughnuts were delightful
Eric's enchiladas were excellent
Freddy's fondue was flippin' fantastic

Gloria's gateau was great
Hayley's honey was heavenly
Izzy's ice was insightful

Jerry's jelly was... just...
Katie's kale was kinda kooky
Larry's lamb was laughable

Martin's macaroni was marvellous
Naomi's nut roast was nae bad
Olivia's olives were outstanding

Patrick's pizza was particularly pleasing
Quincy's quiche was quality
Ron's rolls were rancid

Sally's salad was sensational
Terry's trifle was terrific
Ulrich's udon was unbelievable

Vanessa's Viennetta was vexing
Walter's walnuts were wonderful
Xavier's xacuti was xhilarating

Yanni's yams were yummy
Zara's zucchini was zesty

A PERSON CALLED MORNING

There once was a person called Morning
Who found the evening quite boring
All they wanted was bed
To rest their head
So when they woke they wouldn't be yawning

THE FREEZING SNOWMAN

The snowman felt freezing,
he didn't know what do.
He had a hat and a scarf
and some gloves on too.

But the snow kept falling
and the wind got colder,
the chill kept rising from
his toe to his shoulder.

As the sun went down
and the moon came up
the snowman decided
enough was enough.

He left the white field
shuffling two frozen feet,
got the bus to the airport
and flew to Spain for a week.

COUNTLESS CREEPY EYES

Eva found a spider
climbing up the wall.
She giggled as it wiggled,
she wasn't scared at all.

She loved its legs all hairy,
its countless creepy eyes.
She loved its web all shiny
and how it gobbled flies.

LONG BEARD

I knew a man with a beard
as long as the man was tall.
It was black, white and grey
and as strong as a brick wall.

Whenever he ate dinner
like eggs or beans or stew,
blobs would stick to the hairs
like they were made out of glue.

He would carry things inside it
like his wallet, phone and keys.
He'd let dogs sleep inside it
and squirrels, mice and bees.

But walking around was tough,
he couldn't see the floor below.
And if he wasn't wearing shoes
the beard would tangle in his toes.

GIRAFFE

GIRAFFE.
Your neck looks like a cobbled path.
You clearly stand out in freshly cut grass.

GIRAFFE.
Your spots look like brass.
It's a shame you'll never fit inside the bath.

GIRAFFE.
Your supermarkets must have the tallest staff.

GIRAFFE.
You have no voice, but can you laugh?
Which leg do you use to pass a football?
Having four must mean you rarely fall.
I must admit, your tail is cool.
How big is your secondary school?
Wait, what? These don't rhyme at all with

GIRAFFE!

SHOOTING THROUGH THE SKY

Every time there was a plane
shooting through the sky

Frank would raise his hand
to wave and shout *BYE BYE!*

He wondered where it was going
and who was inside.

Were they travelling far away
or just up there for a ride?

He'd yell out all his questions
but the passengers never replied,

none of them could hear him
as they were flying just too high.

So Frank would stick his arms out
like two wings stretching wide

and zoom around the city
going *NYEERRRRM* as he went by.

HELPFUL CREATURES

When things were tough
the kangaroo knew what to do.

When things were rough
the cockatoo knew what to do.

When things got bad
the cuckoo knew what to do.

When things got sad
the Emu knew what to do.

When things felt low
the cockapoo knew what to do.

When things felt slow
the galloping gnu knew what to do.

When I got cross
the tippity-too knew not what to do
(because the tippity-too does not exist, it's true).

When I got lost
it was you who knew what to do.

IF TREES

If trees could talk, would they bark?

If trees could walk, would they leave?

If trees could leave, would they branch out far?

If trees could cheer, would they root for me?

HAVE YOU EVER HEARD OF THE PLANET?

Have you ever heard of the planet
made of crisps and tasty sweets?
It has rain clouds stuffed with orange juice
and chocolate bars the size of leeks.

Have you ever heard of the planet
with an ocean filled with games?
The fish play football, chess and pool
and know each other's names.

Have you ever heard of the planet
with a moon made out of laughter?
Its the kind of place with lots of smiles
and people living happily ever after.

Have you ever heard of the planet
the one with joy not water in its lakes?
Wait, you've never heard of that planet?
Me neither, doesn't it sound great?!

BRIGHT AND PROUD

Butterfly wings are full of colour
Reds, yellows, greens, swirl into each other
When they flap up and down
They shine brightly and proud
And without them the world would be duller

A CARPENTER CALLED KEV

The carpenter was super skilled,
he'd make all sorts out of wood.
Name it and he'd make it,
he really was that good.

But one day Kev doubted himself,
he thought *I can't do anything.*
His best mate Malc reminded him,
Look at the joy you bring:

You make chairs for us to sit on,
tables for us to eat.
You sculpt animals from tree trunks,
I think you're pretty neat.

I wish I could make pigs out of twigs
or turn a branch into a rake.
I'd love to make a car from bark
or turn some oak into a gate!

Kev smiled from ear to ear,
felt his confidence grow back.
He grabbed his tools and got to work
and made Malc a wooden hat.

THE END

A book will never end
if you do not want it to,
like a very best friend
it will always be with you.

A book will never end
once it lives inside your head,
all the tales will blend
while you dream inside your bed.

Acknowledgements

Thanks to Michelle Moloney King at Beir Bua for the incredible work she's doing for poets. *Fish Fingers, Bumble, I Know! I Know!* and *Anne Onion* were first published in *Kidstuff* by Dreich.

Thanks Mum, Dad, Burt, Janet, and Father Christmas for all of the pens and notebooks under the Christmas tree with my name on.

Thanks to Frank for pointing his little fingers at the world's interesting corners.

And thanks to Caroline for always reminding me how important it is to find the time and space to do what you enjoy.

About the Author

Carl Burkitt likes telling tales. He tells long tales, short tales, silly tales, sad tales, and tells them online, behind a mic, in books, in schools, and on the sofa with his young family. *Elephants Sleep in Bunk Beds* is Carl's debut children's collection.

Praise for the Author

"Poems of joy, wonder and silliness. Carl is a master of showing us what words and imaginations can do."

- Erin Bolens, Poet

"This book is the beautiful, witty, and wonderful world of Carl Burkitt's brain. It's full of flowers, flamingoes and downright funny jokes. It made me laugh, weep and let out little sighs of joy"

- Lewis Buxton, Poet

Maze

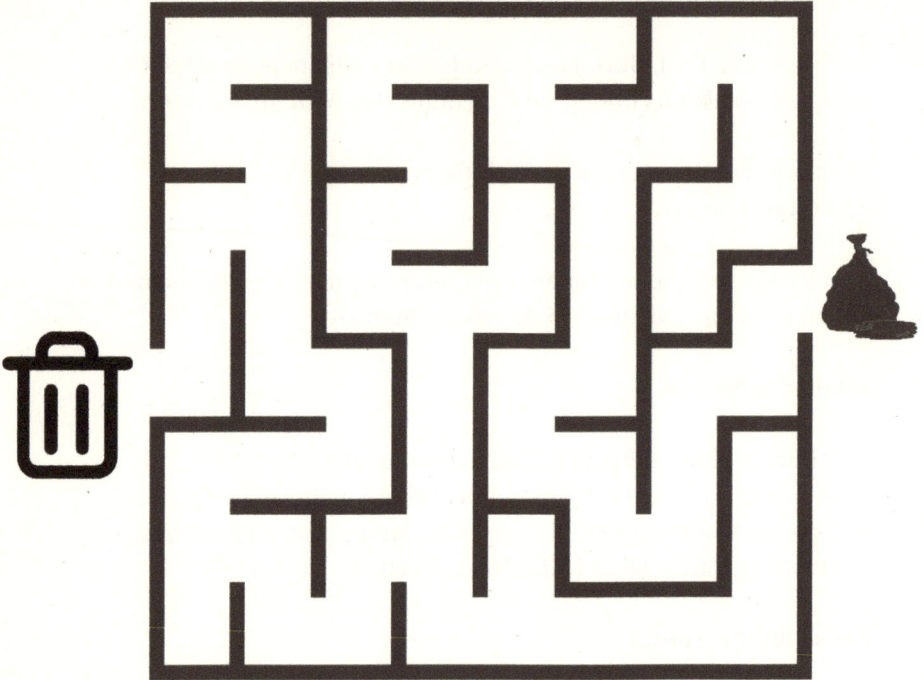